MEGA
AND THE WEATHER WITCH

Two Stories

Written by
ALLEN MORGAN

Illustrated by
VLADYANA KRYKORKA

Vladyana

The Weather Witch

Once upon a time not so long ago a girl named Megan made a lemonade stand in front of her house in Toronto. It was getting towards the end of July and the weather was dry and hot. There hadn't been rain for more than a week, not a single drop, and there wasn't a cloud in sight. The flowers were dying, the grass was too, and the road was soft and sticky as glue. Cars blew off their radiator caps, dogs took naps in the shade for hours and everyone showered with the cold tap up full.

So business was brisk in the lemonade trade and Megan's stand was doing okay. She squeezed it up fresh and she kept it ice cold - once word got around about how nice it was, people dropped in from all over. Her parents bought some and the neighbours did too, a cabby drank one, his fare had two, a postie stopped by on her way past the stand and a rich-looking woman in a stretch limousine sent over her chauffeur to fetch back a cup for her puppy. It all seemed to be quite exciting at the time, but it was nothing compared to what happened next.

"Ahoy down there! "a voice called out from high overhead.

A rope ladder suddenly dropped from the sky. The bottom rung stopped just in front of Megan's nose and swung to and fro as it hung in the air. It was very peculiar, but when Megan looked up she soon realized it was far more strange than she'd thought. The ladder swung down from a huge balloon and a woman was swinging there too!

"Hi there ducks, I'm in luck to find you!" she called as she climbed into view.

Lemonade

The woman was tall and dressed all in black. She wore black buckle shoes with points at the toes, a long black dress and black dappled stockings. Her nose was hooked and her chin was crooked; her hair was long and midnight black like her hat which was tall and quite pointed on top. Megan was impressed.

"You're a witch I bet," she whispered in awe.

"I am," said the witch. "But don't bet too much till you know which kind."

"Are there different kinds?"

"Why of course my dear. There are good witches, bad witches, water witches, sand witches, all kinds and all sorts in all shapes and sizes. They each do something different and they do it different ways."

"Which kind are you?"

"I'm a Weather Witch. I fly through the sky in my weather balloon and work with the clouds."

"Can you please make it rain for us sometime soon?" Megan asked her.

"I'll try," she replied. "I'll go out tonight in my weather balloon and do what I can. You can help too. I'll come by later and pick you up. In the meantime I need some lemonade."

"Sure," Megan said. "I just squeezed some lemons for a brand-new batch. I'll add the sugar and..."

"Oh please don't add sugar," the Weather Witch told her.

"But it's much too sour the way it is now," Megan explained. "Sip some and see."

She poured out a cup. The Weather Witch tried it and made a face.

"Phew! That sure is sour!" she agreed. "I think it needs a few more lemons though..."

"*More* lemons?" Megan asked in surprise.

"Absolutely!" the Weather Witch told her. "The lemonade's not for me, my dear; it's for my two bats and that's just how they like it. Everything's backwards with bats you know, what's sour to our taste is sweet to them. Maybe you better put three lemons in, just to be on the safe side."

Megan shrugged and squeezed them in. She filled two cups for the Weather Witch, who balanced them both on the brim of her hat and started back up the ladder again.

"Toodaloo caribou, I'll be back for you later on tonight," she called as she climbed out of sight.

The Weather Witch unhitched her weather balloon and soon she was flying away. Megan sighed as she watched her go.

"No-one'll ever believe this at all!" she thought.

She wasn't quite sure she believed it herself. But later that night when she went up to bed she decided to stay awake for a while just in case it was true. She went to the window and gazed at the sky. The last light of day was beginning to fade and give way to the coming night. But there wasn't a single cloud in sight. There wasn't any sign of a weather balloon either.

"Maybe I made it all up," she said as she went back to bed.

Megan woke up again later that night. The stars were out and a full moon was rising. The city was quiet. Nothing stirred and the only sound that Megan heard was a lonely tapping as something soft bumped on the window pane. All of a sudden she saw what it was - a rope ladder!

"Ahoy down there!" a familiar voice called. "Climb up and come aboard!"

"I knew you'd come," Megan said when she reached the basket underneath the balloon.

"I knew I would too," said the Weather Witch as she unhitched the anchor from Megan's roof. "Hold onto your bongos, we're going to take off!"

The balloon rose up and soon they were flying across the night sky. The view was beautiful. The moon turned the city all silvery white and the street lights made streaks of gold. Megan felt marvellously happy.

"I've always wanted to know a real live witch," she said with a grin. "Where's your black cat?"

"I never use cats for my weather spells," the Weather Witch said." I have bats for that. Wizards use lizards but I always say a bat's more dependable. With bats you know where you stand."

As she spoke two bats came flying in. One was skinny; the other was fat and both were wearing dandelion rings. They circled the balloon for a moment or two, then the fat one threw his flower ring around the Witch's hat. When that was done he grabbed the brim and hung there upside down. The skinny bat stayed in the air a bit longer to show off his chain of dandelions.

"I made it for me, I hope you don't like it," he told the Weather Witch.

"You talked!" exclaimed Megan.

"No way, not me," the skinny bat said. "You're crazy!"

"And stupid too," the fat bat added.

"Am not!" Megan told him.

"Hey don't look at me, I can't hear a thing. My eyes are closed!" the fat bat replied and he stared at Megan with big round eyes that didn't blink once.

"I'm so glad they like you!" the Weather Witch said.

"They do?" Megan asked. "Are you sure?"

"Absolutely. The bats always say the opposite of what they mean. If they say you're stupid it means you're smart. If they say you're crazy it means you're okay. It comes from hanging upside down. They get everything backwards, but that's just what you need for weather spells, they go backwards you know so the bats are quite good at them. Isn't that right, dears?"

"Buzz to that," the skinny bat told her.

"Go eat a baloney!" the fat bat said.

"You see," said the Weather Witch happily. "That's bats for you. With bats you know where you stand!"

They flew through the sky for an hour or two before finally finding some clouds. But the trouble was, the ones that they found weren't all that large.

"There can't be much rain inside any of these," Megan decided.

"One at a time they aren't worth a dime," the Weather Witch agreed. "You need more than one lemon to make lemonade and you've got to know how to squeeze. Clouds work the same, you just put them together. So what do you think, let's take the plunge."

And then without fuss or further ado she threw herself over the side of the basket. Megan gasped.

"Come back!" she cried, but she knew it was much too late.

Or was it? The Weather Witch suddenly reappeared in the air astride a cloud.

"Come on ducks! It's time to ride!" she called as she galloped away.

The cloud she was riding was shaped like a horse and it acted a lot like one too. Megan watched as the Weather Witch started to herd all the clouds back to the city. One small cloud remained behind. Megan knew just what to do. She put her fingers between her teeth and whistled loudly. As soon as she did the cloud drifted over and hovered beside the balloon. Slowly and carefully Megan climbed on. The cloud was soft, yet surprisingly firm. It adjusted its shape as she sat on its back, and in no time at all it looked very much like a pony.

"Now how do I make you go I wonder?" Megan asked herself.

No sooner had the thought formed inside her head than the cloud leaped up in the sky overhead with a breathtaking jump that dumped Megan's stomach down near her toes. Megan threw her arms around the cloud's neck and squeezed with her knees for dear life.

"It's not so much the starting I need," she told herself grimly. "It's more the stopping I miss."

And just as the thought flew out of her head, the cloud stopped still.

"You can hear me thinking!" Megan cried. "Come on, let's ride, there's work to be done!"

So Megan and the Weather Witch rounded up all the clouds they could find and herded them back to Toronto.

And when they finally got back to town the Weather Witch used a long rope lasso to tie all the clouds into one huge pile.

"Time for you two to get to work," the Weather Witch told the bats.

"No way," cried the skinny one. "I'm taking a break!"

"Get lost," said the fat bat. "I'm having a nap!"

They flew straight over to the bulging clouds and hovered above them, whistling and squawking and carrying on like a calliope caught in a windstorm.

Soon they came back to the balloon again.

"We forgot all the words," the skinny bat told them.

"And we said them all wrong," the fat bat said.

"Aren't they adorable," the Weather Witch whispered. "They love doing spells and they do them so well."

Then she pulled on the cloud rope as hard as she could and Megan did too. The clouds all turned from grey to black as they squeezed together. Then all of a sudden Crrrrack! - a bolt of lightening came shooting out and a roll of thunder came rumbling after.

"Keep pulling, pull harder," the Weather Witch cried. "The clouds in the middle are starting to break!"

Suddenly it began to rain. Torrents of water poured out of the clouds and down to the city below.

"Way to go!" Megan shouted. "It's raining! We did it!"

"So what's the big deal?" the skinny bat asked.

"Yeah," said the fat bat and he made a rude noise. "I've seen better action in the car wash."

When the Weather Witch dropped Megan off at her house, she promised to come back and give her a ride in the weather balloon any night she liked. And this is the song she taught Megan to sing when she wanted to go for a ride:

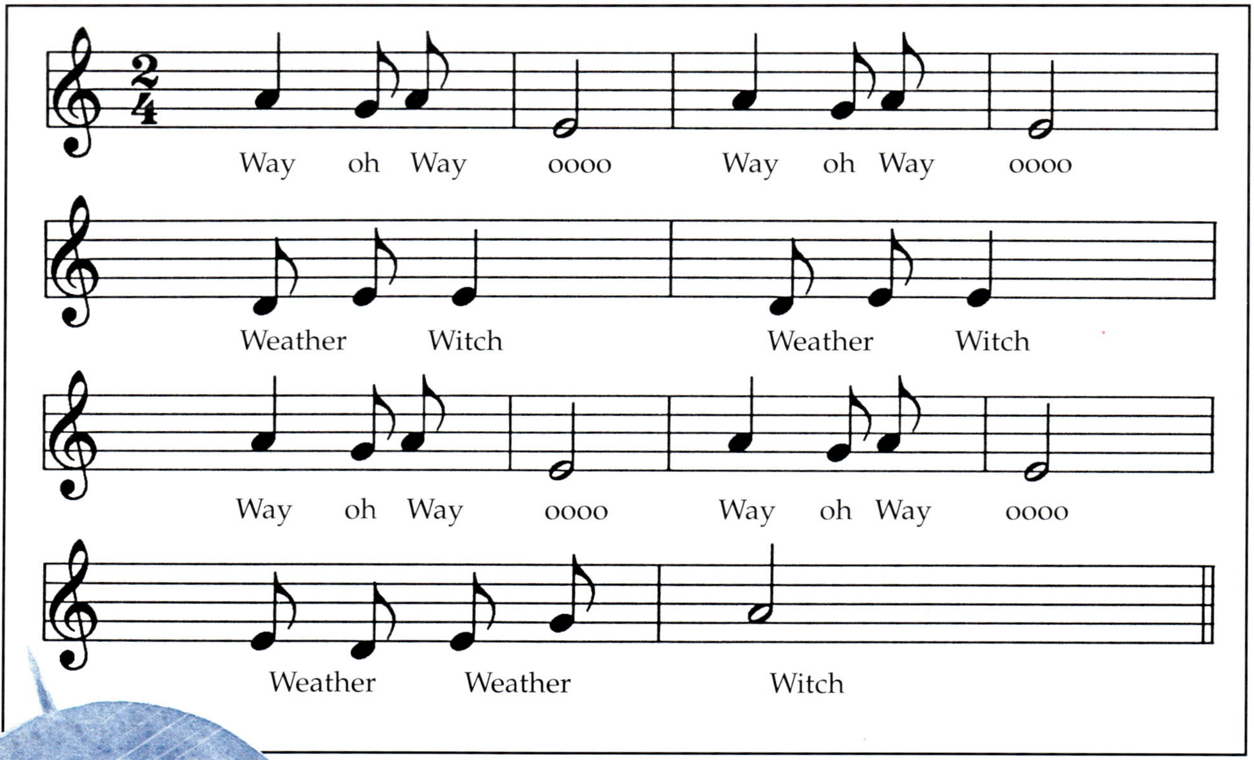

So ever after that when Megan didn't feel like going to sleep she just called the song by her bedroom window and the Weather Witch came in her weather balloon. Sometimes they gathered the rain clouds in, sometimes they drove them away instead. And sometimes they went for a long ride together and stayed out all night till the first light of dawn, travelling off across the night sky to see what lies hidden beyond the horizon where the moon and the stars and our dreams are born.

The Bats And The Statue Parade

All that fall and throughout the winter, Megan and the Weather Witch had lots of fun together. But during the spring things got very busy and Megan forgot all about her new friend. Then late one night near the end of May, the Weather Witch flew to Megan's house without even waiting to hear her song.

"Wake up ducks, we've got things to do," she called as she threw down the ladder.

Megan got dressed just as soon as she could and climbed up to the weather balloon.

"Hi!" she said when she finally arrived. "I haven't seen you guys for days and days. How have you been?"

"Goodbye! We stink! And so do you!" the fat bat said.

"We're sad to see you," the skinny bat squeaked.

Megan was glad to hear it because she knew the bats always said the opposite of what they really meant.

"I missed you too," she told them.

"Hello jello-face, we have to stay. We ain't coming back; we'll be gone for days," the fat bat cried.

"We'll never see you ever again, especially downtown," the skinny one called, then they both flew away.

"Aren't they cute? They're very excited," the Weather Witch said. "We're celebrating their birthday tonight. There's going to be a parade."

"A parade?" asked Megan. "For their birthday?"

"Well actually it's not their real birthday. You know the way bats are, everything backwards. Their real birthday is six months away, in November."

"Then how do they rate a parade?" Megan said.

"The parade's not for them," the Weather Witch explained. "It's for Queen Victoria. The bats think she's nice so they like to join in! They've just gone off now to invite some friends. They'll meet us downtown later on."

"That's right!" Megan said. "I remember it now. Tomorrow's Victoria Day. But I sort of forget, who was she exactly?"

"She was the Queen of England a long time ago," said the Weather Witch. "And we use her birthday to celebrate whoever it is that's the Queen today, or the King as the case may be."

Now maybe you know this or maybe you don't, but whenever they have a parade in Toronto they march down University Avenue. They do it because it's so straight and wide and it has two sides with flowers in between and all the statues you could possibly want are there to watch it go by. So Megan was starting to feel excited. She didn't know how the parade would be, still even so, she was sure there'd be lots to see. But strangely enough when they finally arrived, the place was completely deserted! Not a sight nor a sound of a single soul - even the squirrels were asleep.

"I thought there was going to be a parade," Megan said.

"Victoria Day begins after midnight," the Weather Witch told her. "The parade doesn't start until after then too."

Megan looked at her watch. It was five to twelve.

"Everyone seems to have gone to bed. There's no-one to watch it but us," she said.

"We didn't fly all this way just to watch," said the Weather Witch. "If you come to *this* parade you have to be in it."

"It looks to me like we'll have to be the whole parade ourselves," Megan told her.

"I wouldn't say that," the Weather Witch said. "There's more to the world than meets the eye and your nose knows more smells than it tells."

"But you and I are the only ones here," Megan insisted. "Unless you start counting the statues."

"Exactly! They're just the ones that I'm counting on!"

"But statues can't be in a parade!" Megan laughed.

"Whyever not?" asked the Weather Witch.

"They're not alive!"

"Oh they're not? Is that so? And how do you know?"

"Because statues can't move," Megan explained.

"What you mean is you've never seen them. But statues have legs, so why can't they use them! They've all got ears, so why can't they hear? And if they've got eyes they can certainly see!"

"They've got mouths too," said Megan. "But I've never heard one speak!"

"Maybe you haven't been listening dear," the Weather Witch replied.

She led Megan over to a large statue of a man on a horse.

"King Edward," said Megan as she read the plaque. "Was Edward the King when Victoria was Queen?"

"He was her son. He got to be king when she was done," the Weather Witch explained. "Now that he's dead we all call him King Eddie, at least to his statue. Statues don't stand on ceremony much - they stand around enough as it is."

The statue in question didn't seem to want to stand on its pedestal either. A nearby clock began tolling the midnight hour, and when the first bell sounded the horse gave a twitch. Megan was amazed.

"It moved!" she gasped. "It's coming alive!"

"It's alive already," the Weather Witch said. "It just isn't standing as still as it used to. Statues can move just like you and me, but they stand still so long they forget that they can. They sometimes need someone to help them remember. Come on, let's wake King Eddie up. I know a good waking-up spell."

"I thought you only did weather spells," Megan whispered.

"Well, I dabble a bit in other things too," admitted the Weather Witch. "The bats always like to invite the statues to their birthday do, so I do what I can."

She reached down and picked up two sticks from the ground. Then she sang this song as she clicked them together. Megan joined in and sang too.

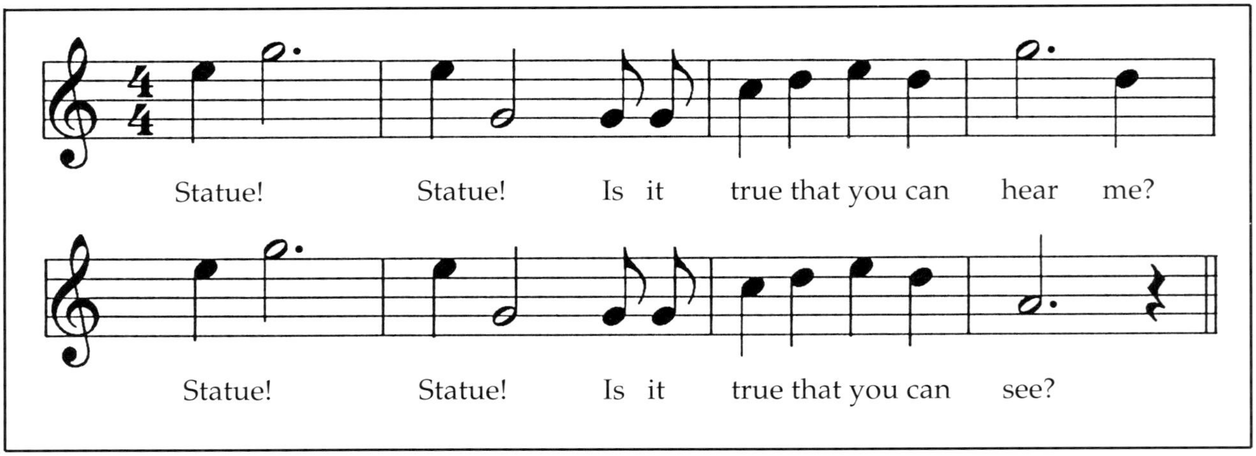

And sure enough as they sang the song, King Eddie opened his eyes. He blinked them twice and wiggled his nose. Then all of a sudden he sneezed.

"Ah!" he sighed contentedly. "You have no idea how good that feels, my nose has been tickling for months!"

VR

"Good evening to you your majesty," the Weather Witch said and she made a small curtsy. "It's time now to start the parade."

"It is?" said King Eddie. "It's May already? Are the other statues awake?"

"No," Megan said. "You're the only one."

"Then we'd better go wake them. Come on, let's go!"

King Eddie reached down to pick Megan up and he gave her a seat on his saddle. The Weather Witch fed his horse sugar lumps, then she led them away to the other statues. King Eddie and Megan helped sing the song, and together they woke up Sir John A. MacDonald, two statues in togas, and even the bust of Toronto's first mayor. His name was MacKenzie and they had to carry him all night long because he was only a head you see and he didn't have a leg to stand on.

They continued around the Parliament Buildings until they finally found the statue of Queen Victoria herself. She was fast asleep on her massive throne, just snoring away. They sang her the statue song three times through, but it didn't do too much good.

"Wake up mum, your birthday has come," King Eddie called out just as loud as he could.

Victoria didn't hear him at all. She went right on snoring like she ruled the world, or at least the waves.

"She's fond of a snooze," King Eddie explained." She's getting quite old now so what can you say? She's out like a light brigade."

"So what'll we do?" Megan asked her two friends.

"Let's start the parade," the Weather Witch said. "We'll make so much noise coming by her throne, she'll wake up herself on her own."

It seemed like a good idea all right so King Eddie and Megan and the Weather Witch went off down University Avenue to wake all the statues up. It wasn't too hard and it didn't take long. The statues were glad it was time to parade, they'd been watching so many go by all year they were dying to march themselves. Old Adam Beck was the last one they found.

"We're going to go yell at the Queen," they explained when he finally woke up and could move again.

"Count me in lads," he said with a grin.

"Get ready! Get ready!" King Eddie called out. "All you statues line up two by two. We'll march on up the Avenue! Step smartly and follow me!"

Everyone did and needless to say the parade that they made was amazing to see! The Angel of Victory flew high overhead with a garland crown while King Eddie and Megan led the way on the ground down below. There were soldiers and lions and John A. MacDonald - but the best was still yet to come! They'd hardly gone more than a block and a half when the bats arrived with a massive flock of plastic flamingos they'd gathered together from various lawns all around the town. They'd found a number of garden gnomes too and a big metal sculpture by Henry Moore from in front of the Art Gallery.

"We're not very smart but we know what we hate," the fat bat claimed.

"This rock's pretty small, but it sure can't roll!" the skinny bat squeaked.

The Weather Witch laughed. "The bats are great fans of Henry Moore, They like to fly through all his holes," she told Megan.

The numbers swelled and the throng grew and grew as it marched along the Avenue. When they made the circle around Queens Park, the Weather Witch stopped at the Royal Museum and released a few dinosaurs too.

"I know they're not actually statues," she said. "But they promised they'd try not to eat anyone and the bats think they're really neat."

"By all means let them come," said King Eddie. "They can help us make noise and we'll need lots of that to wake up my mum."

When the parade reached the base of Victoria's throne they sang Happy Birthday and God Save The Queen. Everyone yelled and the dinosaurs roared. Victoria stopped snoring and opened her eyes.

"What a lovely surprise," she said sleepily. "I'm glad you could come, won't you stay and have tea?"

As you probably know or have already guessed, peanut butter sandwiches with watercress are the very best thing to serve for tea, especially if it's for royalty. Victoria had some underneath her throne, so she passed them around and then poured out some tea made from licorice drops and blackberry chews and various other lugubrious things.

"Please have some, do," she told them all. "I brew it myself from whatever is left on the candy shelf after Halloween."

The Weather Witch brought out an unbirthday cake that she'd baked using lemons and limes. It was very sour. She didn't use sugar or anything sweet, so even though no-one else liked it at all, the bats both thought it was really good and they ate it all up on their own.

And when they were through devouring cake, the bats sang themselves a birthday song.

"Stupid Birthday to us - This party's a bust
I'm ugly as a catcher - You smell like a bus!"

When tea was all done they had plenty of games, they played British-Bulldog and raced in relays. Red-Rover-Come-Over was popular too, but the very best favourite was Statue-Tag. Everyone had a wonderful time and when the party broke up at dawn, they asked Megan to come again next year.

The eastern sky was beginning to brighten as the Weather Witch flew back to Megan's house. The bats were so tired from all the fun they fell fast asleep hanging upside down with great big frowns on their faces.

"Does anyone else but the bats and you know that the statues have a parade each year on Victoria Day?" Megan asked the Weather Witch.

"No they don't," she replied. "And they'll never guess. By the time all the people get out of bed and come back downtown to work again, the statues will all have gone back to their places. They'll be standing quite still and they won't make a move till it's time to wake up again next year."

And as it turned out she was right about that. Nobody noticed and nobody knew that the statues were real and they really could move. But Megan knew and now that you do, if you happen to be in Toronto someday walking along University Avenue, pick up some sticks and click them together. And then if you sing the statue song too, maybe the statues will hear you. They might give a twitch or perhaps blink an eye, and if they do that be sure to say how many days left till Victoria Day so the statues will know how much longer they still have to wait.

To babi Mila for making impossible things happen - V.
For Bear - A.

Canadian Cataloguing in Publication Data

Morgan, Allen 1946 -
Megan and the weather witch

ISBN 1-895092-03-5

I. Krykorka, Vladyana. II. Title

PS8576.0642M43 1993 jC813'. 54 C92-095351-4
PZ7.M67Me 1993

Distributed by:
Oasis Press
38 Nina St.
Toronto, Ont.
M5R 1Z4

Layout design: Taunyee Robbins
Vladyana's photo: Tom Arban
Colour separations: Chromascan, Ottawa, Ontario
Printed in Canada by Hignell Printing Ltd.